THE SUMERIANS

THE SUMERIANS

ELAINE LANDAU

THE CRADLE OF CIVILIZATION
THE MILLBROOK PRESS
BROOKFIELD, CONNECTICUT

For Michael Brent Pearl
a modern-day wonder

Cover photograph courtesy of Erich Lessing/
Art Resource, NY

Photographs courtesy of © Tor Eigeland: pp. 2-3, 16,
51; © Peter Schmid/SuperStock: p. 18; © Erich Lessing/
Art Resource, NY: pp. 22-23, 34 (both), 36, 41;
Giraudon/Art Resource, NY: p. 25; Scala/Art Resource,
NY: pp. 26-27, 31, 42, 46; The Granger Collection, New
York: p. 40; Rijksmuseum van Oudheden (neg. no. VF
1012): p. 45; © 1983 The Metropolitan Museum of Art,
The Fletcher Fund, 1963 (63.74-ANE): p. 49.

Library of Congress Cataloging-in-Publication Data
The Sumerians / Elaine Landau.
p.   cm.–(Cradle of civilization)
Includes bibliographical references and index.
Summary: Examines Sumer, the earliest advanced society
to emerge from Mesopotamia, including its contributions
in written language, farming, art, and science.
ISBN 0-7613-0215-8 (lib. bdg.)
1. Sumerians–Juvenile literature.   [1. Sumerians.]
I. Title. II. Series: Landau, Elaine. Cradle of civilization.
DS72.L32   1997
935–dc21   96-46898   CIP   AC

Published by The Millbrook Press, Inc.
2 Old New Milford Road
Brookfield, Connecticut 06804

CONTENTS

Chapter 1
In the Beginning
9

Chapter 2
As Sumer Grew
14

Chapter 3
Writing, Education, and Law
33

Chapter 4
Sumer at Work
39

Chapter 5
The Twilight Years
48

Important Dates
53

Notes
55

Glossary
57

Further Readings
59

Index
61

THE SUMERIANS

IN THE BEGINNING

Thousands of years ago there were no cities, countries, or governments as we know them today. Instead, small bands of people roamed the Earth living off the land. They were hunters and gatherers who were always on the move in search of wild game and fish as well as fruits and nuts to eat. These individuals didn't think of themselves as having a homeland. They were nomadic, or wandering, groups guided in their travels by the need to find food to survive.

No one knows precisely how or why things changed. What made some people trade the freedom to follow the animal herds for the strenuous task of tilling the soil? Although there are no definite answers, a number of theories have been suggested.

Historians note that at first just a few people may have separated from the wandering band. These were probably the weaker or smaller individuals who might have found it difficult to keep up with the rest. In addition, those who had been scorned or were unhappy with the group for some reason may have started to drop out as well.

It is also thought that women possibly played an important role in families settling down. Giving birth to and caring for young children while on the go must have been extremely difficult. Once women realized that remaining in one place would be best for both their offspring (children) and families, they may have been a powerful force behind this change of lifestyle.

There are numerous other unanswered questions as well. For example, when did the process of growing one's own food or planting and harvesting crops begin? Did a specific incident or change in the environment spur it on? Could some gathered seeds stored outdoors have accidentally taken root and become the first crop field? Or did the first "crops" spring up after some seeds left in a rubbish heap sprouted?

Naturally, this change didn't occur all at once. First, small groups of people settled down together forming early villages that eventually grew into towns and cities. As these communities continued over the years, they changed. Societies complete with a written language, a code of law, and advanced technologies developed.

One of the places this first occurred was an area in what is now the Middle East known as Mesopotamia—a land between where the Tigris and Euphrates rivers empty into the Persian

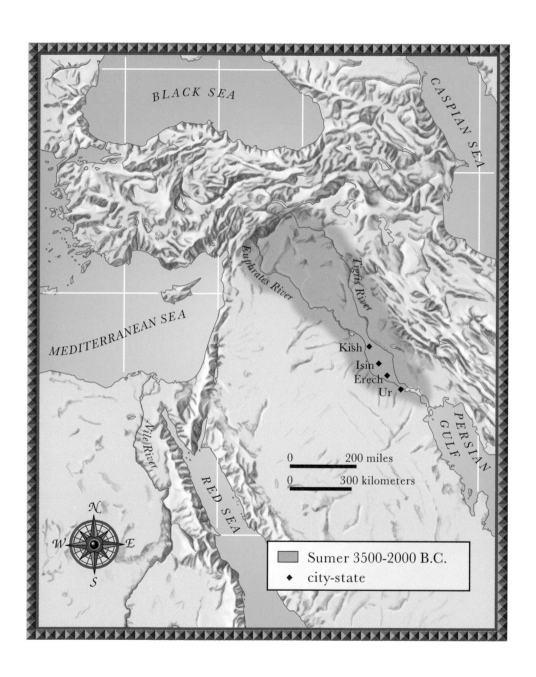

Gulf.[1] There on a hot, dry, windswept plain, now referred to as a "cradle of civilization," some of the earliest cultures arose. Among these was Sumer, which occupied 10,000 square miles (26,000 square kilometers) in southern Mesopotamia. Sumer later became Babylonia. A third accomplished Mesopotamian civilization was Assyria, an area on the upper Tigris River in northern Mesopotamia.

The borders between these ancient areas were not always precisely drawn. Wars, political takeovers, and population shifts all served to intermingle the various peoples in the vicinity. Yet these three cultures remain distinct for their important contributions to the world. Ancient Mesopotamians invented the wheel, studied the stars and other heavenly bodies, and achieved important developments in mathematics, medicine, and architecture. They built cities, made advances in art and literature, and were the first people to develop a legal code.

For many years little was known about ancient Mesopotamia. Rain, floods, shifting sands, and other natural occurrences had erased its narrow, winding streets and its courtyards, religious towers, and magnificent palaces. But by the mid-nineteenth century, archaeologists unearthed the clay tablets, pottery, tools, and building ruins of the Mesopotamians. To accomplish this, archaeological teams dug through huge mounds of soil, stripping away numerous layers of earth. Photographers took pictures of any articles found, while archaeologists interpreted when and how the various items were used. Specialists in ancient languages translated the writings on clay tablets, providing even more information on societies of the past. These clues enabled them to piece together a fascinating picture of the extremely advanced and industrious peoples who once inhabited this "cradle of civilization."

AS SUMER GREW

Until about 5000 B.C. when its first settlers entered the marshy area near the Persian Gulf, no one lived in Sumer. These marsh dwellers, known as Ubaidians, gave the area a valuable early foundation. Despite the barren surroundings, the Ubaidians made the most of the available resources. To farm the dry land, they channeled any water overflow from the surrounding Tigris and Euphrates rivers to their fields and gardens. Irrigating the land in that manner, they were able to produce numerous crops. The Ubaidians fashioned pots, plates, jugs, and various types of farm equipment out of the baked mud and clay from the rivers. Their housing was practical as well. They lived in huts made of dried marsh reeds woven into mats and plastered together with mud.

For a time the Ubaidians lived in the region undisturbed. Before long another group challenged their sole right to the area. Semitic tribes (descendants of the legendary Shem, eldest son of Noah) from the Syrian Desert and Arabian Peninsula raided the Ubaidians' settlements, taking anything of value. However, other members of these tribes came in peace, hoping to join the Ubaidians to enhance their own lifestyle.

As the years passed, Ubaidians and Semitic tribe members intermarried (married one another), providing a ripe setting for the arrival of the Sumerians in about 3500 B.C. Historians aren't certain where the Sumerians originally were from. Some think they may have been from the east or northeast of the region, while others believe they came from Central Asia, having traveled through what today is Iran.

But regardless of their origin, as the early settlers in Sumer prospered, their families grew. Having more children to help with the farmwork meant that a greater amount of land could be cultivated, yielding increased crops. Before long, larger homes were needed for these thriving families. In place of the reed huts of the past, they constructed mud-brick homes with a number of rooms. Active communities sprang up as people realized that families could benefit by working together toward a common goal.

But despite these efforts, living in small scattered villages left these individuals vulnerable to attacks from raiding nomadic bands. For their own protection, they joined together in larger settlements. Many Sumerians also moved farther inland since the attacks usually came from directly across the borders. Slowly, Sumerian settlements began to turn from open villages

to large walled-in cities. This trend continued until only massive settlements existed with no small villages in between.

Since they believed that each village and city was protected by a particular deity, or god, the center of every Sumerian city was its temple. An outstanding feature of many of these houses of worship was the ziggurat—a massive pyramid-shaped terrace tower—on top of which the temple itself was built. A typical ziggurat consisted of three to seven levels, or decks. Ziggurats were important to the Sumerians, who believed that these towers connected heaven and Earth. Many temples were designed with huge pillars, and often clay nails with colored nail heads were used to form attractive designs on the building's exterior.

Numerous religious rituals were conducted at the temple. Special prayers were recited and hymns sung at particular times. To ensure that all religious rites were properly performed, a priesthood developed. It began with a handful of well-respected individuals within the community and grew over the years. Under the guidance of these priests, the temples became both the learning and spiritual centers of the community.

The first people to settle in Mesopotamia set up communities in a marshy area along the Persian Gulf between the Tigris and Euphrates rivers. People still live in this area thousands of years later.

A ziggurat, topped with a temple, was an impressive structure and was the center of every Sumerian city.

Besides those in the priesthood, a broad range of other people worked at the temple. They took care of the temple's building and grounds, farmed temple-owned land, tended livestock belonging to the temple, and performed numerous other related tasks.

Additional changes occurred as Sumerian villages grew into productive cities. To keep their greatly increased farming area fertile, advanced irrigation systems were developed. Far-reaching canals were designed and extensive water reservoirs dug and maintained. Such huge projects required the participation of nearly everyone in the community. Families also had to work together to see that water rights were equally distributed and local land boundaries correctly marked.

As the Sumerians' allegiance shifted from the family to the larger community, the need for some form of government became apparent. An official body was necessary to oversee public services, settle disputes, and handle issues affecting the whole town. To fill this gap, Sumerians held public meetings at which officials were democratically appointed to see to these matters. If these people proved unworthy of the public trust, the community could discharge them from their positions.

Although the towns were still somewhat small, this democratically directed form of government met their needs. But as towns grew in size and power, relationships among them became increasingly complex. Rivalries over territory or water rights sometimes erupted, resulting in war among Sumerian cities.

To deal with the threat of attack from other Sumerian cities, each town had to be prepared for war at all times. It was clear that a more extensive form of government was necessary to build a strong and ready army and to devise a comprehensive defense plan. To solve the immediate problem, a strong, capable leader would be picked to handle the crisis. At first such individuals ruled only for a short period of time, resuming their former role in society once the urgent military threat was over. But the Sumerians soon realized that the ever-present danger of war made it impractical to return to their earlier form of government. Men chosen to rule now tended to stay in office for years, eventually becoming all-powerful. Upon their death, the position would automatically be passed on to their sons. These individuals were actually the first kings, and their rise signaled the end of democratic rule in Sumer. In time, the Sumerians even claimed that their kings had been chosen by God.

And many Sumerian kings acted as if this were so. They lived in beautiful palaces well staffed with servants and slaves who satisfied the ruler's every whim. The king and his family ate the best food and wore the finest clothing and jewelry. Even in death, Sumerian leaders were surrounded by riches and people to serve them. Uncovered tombs of Sumerian kings reveal that the rulers were buried with both necessities and luxuries, as well as a number of soldiers and servants, who entered the king's tomb after volunteering to serve him in the next world.

Some of these large grave sites contained the remains of soldiers who had died dressed in full battle gear, in addition to court attendants, servants, and even musicians. Splendidly carved wagons and chariots decorated with golden animals and precious stones were also found in tombs. The animal bones alongside these reveal that beasts to pull the king's chariot and wagons after death were also part of the burial plan.

While still alive, most Sumerian kings did their best to glorify their names on Earth. Besides directing the city's wartime activities, these leaders were also active during Sumer's brief periods of peace. Often Sumerian kings kept a large group of slaves, who were actually wartime captives whose lives had been spared. While Sumer was at peace, the king's slaves were put to work fortifying city walls, repairing irrigation systems, building public structures, and fixing roads. But if a conflict with another city or outside power arose, they served as soldiers.

Slave soldiers were only a small part of the army. Since defense was such a vital part of a Sumerian king's responsibility, a professional army was maintained at all times. These extremely well-disciplined soldiers drilled continuously and were highly trained in various aspects of warfare.

By 3000 B.C., Sumer was made up of more than a dozen cities that functioned as separate states. Although people in these different communities shared a common language and similar customs, the various Sumerian city-states were almost always at war with one another. This internal strife stopped

only for short periods in its history when an outside power threatened Sumer. Once outside rule was overthrown, the various city-states returned to warring against one another.

A number of kings and city-states left their mark on Sumer's tumultuous history. The city-state known as Kish was the first to gain control over all of Sumer. Etana, the king under whom

This enameled panel shows Sumerian warriors and a king from the city-state of Ur, surrounded by the spoils they have collected from a war.

this was first accomplished, ruled in about 3000 B.C. Recovered clay tablets indicate that Etana "stabilized all the land," which meant that in addition to ruling Sumer, he also conquered and controlled nearby territory.[2]

After Etana's reign, Erech, another city-state, emerged as the supreme Sumerian power. Located only about 100 miles

(160 kilometers) southeast of Kish, Erech produced a number of impressive kings. Among these was the famous ruler Gilgamesh, who is believed to have reigned during the twenty-seventh century B.C. Many legends surround this ancient leader. These tales, which undoubtedly have been greatly exaggerated, describe how the king fought in hand-to-hand combat with ferocious wild beasts and always won. There are other stories of his victories over fantastic superhuman characters. Some people think that Gilgamesh may have been the ancient figure on whom the Hercules stories of the Greeks are based.

While tales of Gilgamesh's fantastic powers have never been documented, it is known that his reign was filled with internal conflict and strife. He succeeded in defeating the rival Sumerian city-states of Kish and Ur to rule over Sumer. However, these years of warfare exhausted the country, making it a vulnerable target for outside conquerors. When Sumer was attacked from the east by the Elamites, it readily fell.

Despite numerous attempts, it took Sumer more than a century to regain its independence from foreign rule. But there would still be no peace in Sumer. Its history continued to be one of internal strife interrupted by takeovers by hostile outside forces. In about 2250 B.C., the Gutians, a barbarian horde from the north, overran Sumer. It was a brutal invasion as the Gutians ransacked Sumerian cities, depleting the country's supplies and wealth. Deliverance from the cruel oppressors came in 2120 B.C. from the strength of a Sumerian leader known as

Gilgamesh, a Sumerian ruler from the twenty-seventh century B.C., is the subject of many legends, including those that say he fought wild beasts and always won. Here he is shown holding a lion.

*This milking scene shows the importance
of farming in Sumerian life.*

Utuhegal. Utuhegal was from the city-state of Erech, home of
the famous Sumerian leader Gilgamesh as well as other heroic
kings. Although Utuhegal drove out the Gutians, his reign in
Sumer ended rather abruptly. Just seven years after coming to
power, he was overthrown by Ur-Nammu—one of his own army
generals whom he had allowed to run the city-state of Ur.

When Ur-Nammu and his descendants came to power in
about 2100 B.C., however, they proved to be outstanding leaders. Throughout the century they reunited Sumer, recapturing
much of the greatness and splendor it had lost while dominated by the Gutians. Ur-Nammu poured a great deal of en-

ergy into rebuilding both his home city-state of Ur as well as most of the rest of Sumer. Damaged structures were repaired and new buildings erected.

Ur-Nammu also began a number of social reforms to help make Sumer a just society. He saw to it that merchants, traders, and others in commerce used a fair and accurate system of weights and measures in their dealings. He was also the force behind various regulations that made certain the poor and the weak were not taken advantage of by Sumer's powerful wealthy class. Ur-Nammu was active in other areas as well, working to improve agriculture and commerce throughout the land. But his peacetime projects were continually interrupted by attacks from Sumer's former conquerors, the Gutians, and Ur-Nammu died fighting the enemy on the battlefield.

His son Shulgi's nearly fifty-year reign as king was spectacular. Sumerian poets describe Shulgi as an outstanding fighter, as well as a thinker, city planner, and friend of the arts. During Shulgi's time and that of his successors on the throne, his father's work was finally completed. Shulgi devised Sumer's first legal code, which defined the appropriate penalties for various misdeeds. This code was especially important because the recommended punishments were more humane than those of the past. Rather than be put to death or have an eye or limb taken, for example, the code instead allowed an offender to pay a hefty fine.

Strides in both art and technology during this time further underscored Sumer's importance in the ancient world. Sumerian cities were now quite advanced, consisting of between 10,000 and 50,000 residents. These urban centers had narrow, winding streets that were traveled either by foot or by donkey. The temple undoubtedly remained the most outstanding feature of the city as these structures became more elaborate and magnificent with the passage of time.

A Sumerian city supposedly belonged to the god protecting it. However, although both the temple and the king owned large parcels of land, the residents possessed most of the territory. Private land ownership was important to the Sumerian way of life. Nobles and very wealthy individuals owned large estates, while commoners usually had small plots of farmland. In Sumer's prime, a wide array of occupations was represented, including merchants, artists, teachers, priests, physicians, tradespeople, poets, fishermen, farmers, musicians, and scribes.

Regardless of how a Sumerian earned his living, family life was still extremely important in this society. Parents decided whom their children would marry, with engagements becoming official as soon as the groom presented an appropriate gift to the bride's father. Most couples had children shortly after marrying. Sumerian youths were expected to respect and obey their parents. A stubborn or defiant child could be disinherited. At times extremely needy parents or those heavily in debt sold their offspring into slavery. But for the most part, Sumerian families were close-knit units in which children were highly valued and well treated.

Unlike in some other early societies, Sumerian women enjoyed a degree of independence after marriage. They were permitted to own property, serve as a witness in court, and participate in various types of business dealings. But a woman was still not considered a man's equal. Husbands were able to divorce their wives for little cause, and if a woman was unable to have children her husband could take another wife for that purpose. However, many Sumerian couples in this situation chose to adopt children instead.

Sumerian families wore clothes and built homes that reflected their wealth and standing in society. Regardless of their income, most Sumerian men wore their hair long and parted down the middle and might either have a beard or be clean shaven. Men generally wore long skirts that were partly covered by a large wrap worn over one shoulder, leaving the other bare. While both rich and poor men wore the same style of clothing, the garments of well-to-do Sumerians were made out of luxurious, expensive materials. Women wore long dresses that came down to their ankles and, like the men's garments, only covered one shoulder. Sumerian women of means frequently wore brightly colored garments. They enhanced their appearance with beautiful gold bracelets, earrings, and necklaces set with precious stones. Most Sumerian women wore their hair parted down the middle and in braids fastened around their heads.

The average Sumerian family's house was somewhat small, usually one story. Such structures were generally designed with several rooms surrounding an open courtyard. The homes of wealthy Sumerians tended to be larger and more elaborate. Often these were two stories, with the family's living quarters on the upper level and the kitchen, lavatory, and servants' rooms below. There might also be a private chapel, or prayer room, on a lower level. Beneath the house's foundation lay the family's mausoleum, or tomb, where family members were buried. Some people were buried in cemetery graves on the outskirts

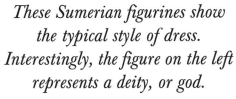

These Sumerian figurines show the typical style of dress. Interestingly, the figure on the left represents a deity, or god.

of the city. Sumerians usually buried their dead with whatever possessions they felt would be useful to their deceased loved ones in the next world.

The development of trade and commerce brought the Sumerians in contact with new materials for building and living. With the increased availability of wood, the people of this nearly treeless land built beds with wooden frames, tables, and stools as well as a variety of chairs and chests with which to furnish their homes. Sumerians also made pots, pans, eating utensils, and numerous household and farming tools out of bronze, copper, and stone. These ingenious people adapted whatever became available to them to enhance their lifestyle and society.

WRITING, EDUCATION, AND LAW

Some historians believe that Sumer's greatest contribution to civilization was the development of a writing system known as cuneiform script. In its earliest form, this method of writing consisted of a series of picture symbols representing both living and nonliving things. Sumerians generally wrote on clay tablets using a wedge-shaped instrument called a stylus. Cuneiform script was developed originally to enable temple officials to keep accurate records. But as Sumer grew into a center of commerce and art, written communication became necessary for many other purposes.

There were thousands of scribes (individuals trained in cuneiform script) in Sumer. Junior scribes were fairly new at this art, while master or high scribes excelled at it. Besides those working at the temple, there were also royal scribes and scribes who held high government positions. Although the Sumerians

Early Sumerian writing (above) consisted of picture symbols. This tablet lists proper names.

Later, cuneiform developed (right). This tablet is the bill of sale for a field and one house, which were paid for in silver.

developed cuneiform script, its use soon spread throughout the region as it was adopted by other early cultures.

Young Sumerians learned cuneiform script in school. Since young people from homes of lesser means had to work the fields or learn a trade at an early age, usually only children from wealthy families were formally educated. But privileged youths attending school often did not look forward to it. Learning to read and write cuneiform script was a difficult, tedious process. Students were required to memorize and copy large numbers of words and symbols. Discipline at these schools was strict. Young people could be caned (hit with a long cane or stick) if they failed to pay attention, made errors, or were late for school. Some students found it hard to be punctual since the school day began at dawn and ended at dusk.

The students' progress and behavior were monitored by a large school staff. The head of the school was known as the "school father." Under him were a number of lesser scholars called "school brothers." School brothers worked directly with the students on a daily basis. It was their job to listen to the students recite their lessons as well as check the students' written work. Others at the school observed and corrected the young people's behavior. There was someone to take attendance each morning and "a man in charge of the whip" to discipline the students.[3]

Although at first Sumer's schools were merely training grounds for future scribes, these schools eventually became much more. Not unlike our colleges and universities, scribe

Under King Shulgi (2094-2047 B.C.), Sumerian society prospered greatly. The king is shown here holding a scale.

schools blossomed into well-rounded centers of learning and culture. Often Sumerian scholars in such fields as botany, astronomy, medicine, and mathematics conducted their research at the schools as well as taught there. Learned scribes at these schools also helped to create Sumer's literature both by writing and collecting an assortment of fables and essays.

The work of scribes was also evident in Sumer's legal system. New legal codes (laws) followed those established by Shulgi who reigned from 2094 to 2047 B.C., and these were written down and referred to. About two centuries after Shulgi's reign, Lipit-Ishtar, a Sumerian king from the city-state of Isin, devised an extensive code of justice. His laws provided penalties for the most common crimes, including trespassing on another's land, the escaping of slaves, and injuring a borrowed farm animal.

Disputes over contracts and agreements regarding land sales, inheritances, and other matters were settled in Sumerian courts of law. Three to four judges heard each case, but these justices did not earn their living within the legal system. Honorable men in the community took turns serving as judges—so a case might be heard by a doctor, scribe, or palace administrator, among others. In some ways, the Sumerians' court processes resembled those of our modern-day courts. Witnesses for both sides were sworn in before testifying, and documents as well as other objects could be introduced as evidence. However, there was no appeals process. Once the verdict in a case was handed down, it could not be legally reversed.

As it had been in the past, the newer Sumerian law was somewhat fair to women, and to a limited extent even slaves were granted rights. Sumerian slaves could own property and were permitted to hold a job after completing their work for their masters. They could use the money they earned to eventually purchase their freedom. Slaves were also allowed to marry free women—this ensured that their children would be free, even if they weren't.

SUMER AT WORK

The Sumerians' many advances earned them an important place in ancient civilization. They were pioneers in architecture, being the first people to use such shapes as the arch and dome in their construction. The Sumerians were also credited with inventing the wheel—and changing commerce and the nature of transportation forever. Wheeled wagons allowed heavy loads to be carried over great distances, permitting building and trade to flourish as never before.

Sumerian society was a rich weave of industry and art. Farming was the stronghold of Sumer's economy. The extensive irrigation system maintained through the years allowed the Sumerians to turn barren land fertile. They even devised a plow that dropped seeds into the furrows it dug. Sumerian farmers carefully monitored the water their crops received as well

Sumerian craftsmen are credited with inventing the wheel. The vehicle they built was probably much like the model shown here, which was made as a burial offering.

as made certain the fields were harvested at the right time. They successfully grew wheat, millet, barley, peas, onions, lettuce, chickpeas, lentils, leeks, turnips, and other vegetables. Fruits such as figs, apples, grapes, and pears, as well as some vegetables, were grown by the Sumerians by a method known as shade gardening. This involved planting in the shade of tall desert palm trees to shield their crops from the blistering sun, harsh winds, and desert sandstorms.

Sumer's crops did more than feed the population. They were also a valuable trading item. The Sumerians traded their extra grain and other rations for wood with which to construct ships and furniture. With this desperately needed resource, they built large sailing vessels and established important trade relations with faraway places such as Africa and India. Traders returned with shiploads of precious metals, various types of wood, exotic foods, and unusual fabrics.

Wool, produced in large quantities by the Sumerians, was another important trade product. Sumerian shepherds raised large flocks of sheep that yielded tons of wool each year. After the sheep were sheared, female slaves spun the fleece by hand and wove it into cloth on looms. The Sumerians also used flax to make linen, but this finer cloth was largely reserved for high priests and royalty.

Wool production was a major industry in Sumerian society. Here a shepherd is shown with one of his lambs.

This beautifully crafted wooden musical instrument may have been made from a previously used piece of wood.

Sumer's various craftspeople were essential to its economy, and nearly every type was represented there. Some of these talented individuals had even come from other lands, attracted by Sumer's thriving economy. Metalworkers in Sumer were busy producing items needed for local industries as well as for home use. Relying on copper, bronze, and tin secured through foreign trade, they made much of the equipment used by farmers and builders. Metalworkers also created the weapons used in wars against rebellious city-states and foreign powers. At times these craftspeople were required to make extra daggers, swords, and shields in a hurry.

Yet it was Sumerian carpenters who had to be especially creative since there was never enough imported wood to meet the local demand. Most of the imported oak, fir, and ebony was reserved for making large trade ships and war chariots. Furniture and other desired wooden items had to be created out of older objects of wood that had been discarded. In this way, the wood from an old table and two chairs might be used to create a bed.

Sumerian basket weavers and leather workers were other busy craftspeople. Basket makers picked reeds from the riverbanks and wove them into a variety of useful objects. They made baskets in which to store things and others to be used as food containers. Basket makers also fashioned tightly woven reeds into small boats.

Leather workers tanned the hides of Sumerian farm animals such as sheep, goats, pigs, and calves along with those of the wild boars and antelopes hunted by Sumerians. They used the newly created leather to make shoes, belts, saddles, waterbags, and shields. Sumerians valued their domesticated farm animals and used these beasts in many different ways. Donkeys and oxen pulled their wagons, transporting both goods and people. Sumerians wove goat-hair rugs, and pork (from pigs) was used as food in numerous Sumerian dishes. Sheep provided fleece for wool, food for the table, and hides for leather. In fact, sheep were so important to the Sumerians that there were more than two hundred words for the animal in their vocabulary.

Sumerian fishermen added to the local food supply as they regularly caught and sold a wide variety of fish. There were also fowlers who hunted game birds to sell for food. At times more than fifty such birds might be delivered to the palace or the home of a wealthy Sumerian for a special feast.

While food providers and craftspeople were important in Sumer, scientists were certainly not unrepresented in this ancient land. Physicians were well respected for their ability to heal the sick. Recovered clay tablets reveal that doctors relied on specific remedies in their work. Many of their potions and salves were made from bark, roots, and plant seeds. Salt, turtle shells, and ground snakeskin were other common remedy ingredients.

To improve a poor-tasting medicine, Sumerian doctors had it placed in a glass of beer before being swallowed. In fact, Sumerians enjoyed large quantities of beer on a daily basis.[4] They made their own brew from the grain they grew, flavoring it with honey, dates, and spices. The beer was considered healthful, and the liquid they produced was actually rich in vitamin B complex. The Sumerians also made wine from their grapes. But as wine was made only once a year and was quite costly, it was not used to take medication.

Surprisingly, early Sumerian doctors were aware of the importance of cleanliness in their practice. Records show that

This carving shows the various stages of brewing beer. The drink produced in Sumer was considered healthful and was used for medicinal purposes as well as for a beverage.

Elaborate jewelry and headdresses were crafted by Sumerian artists for kings and others of great wealth.

they instructed their patients to scrub all wounds and rashes before applying a healing salve. In addition to medical doctors, there were also veterinarians in Sumer who treated sick animals.

Sumerian astronomers studied the stars, while other men of science invented a calendar. Engineers designed and implemented the Sumerians' complex irrigation systems, and mathematicians designed clocks based on the sixty-second minute and the sixty-minute hour—time units we still use today.

The development of science in Sumer was rivaled only by the development of the arts. Music was extremely important to the Sumerians and could be heard at various sites throughout the city. Talented individuals with beautiful voices were greatly admired. Sumerians also played a variety of instruments, including the harp, lyre, drum, and tambourine. Although music was used in some religious rituals, it was also a popular form of entertainment.

Sumerian artists created beautiful daggers, statues, and plaques out of imported gold and copper. Other statues and figurines were carved out of stone. Gold headdresses set with precious gems, gold earrings, and magnificent necklaces have been uncovered from Sumerian royal tombs as well. Although grave robbers had already stolen many of the most valuable items, archaeologists nevertheless learned much about Sumer from what remained. It was indeed an early civilization characterized by industry, creativity, and splendor.

THE TWILIGHT YEARS

Although the Sumerians achieved a great deal, in the end their ability and drive were not sufficient to fend off their warring neighbors. When the Sumerian ruler Ibbi-Sin, the fifth and last descendant of Ur-Nammu, came to power, he faced enemy attacks on more than one front. To the east the Elamites, longtime enemies of the Sumerians, were once again anxious to overrun the country. The difficulty of mounting an ongoing defense against the Elamites was compounded by the attacks of the Amorites, a nomadic people from the west.

Weakened by fighting a double threat, Sumer began to crumble. Ibbi-Sin's rule was further hampered by numerous disloyal army generals and city-state governors. Sensing that Ibbi-Sin would soon be defeated, they often acted out of their own self-interest instead of that of their country. Among them was one of Ibbi-Sin's closest generals, who left his post and broke relations with the king. He declared himself both head of the Sumerian city-state of Isin as well as the new ruler of Sumer.

For a time, Ibbi-Sin was forced to battle this general as well as his enemies outside the country. But he did not have the resources to cope with both internal strife and strikes from two outside powers. His final downfall occurred in about 2006 B.C., when the Elamites demolished his home city-state of Ur, taking him prisoner. However, the Elamites did not rest comfortably in Sumer for long. The Amorites eventually drove them out, firmly establishing themselves in the area. Since that time, the Sumerians ceased to exist as a separate and distinct people and culture.

The importance of war and conquest in Mesopotamia at the time of the Sumerians is evident in the fine craftsmanship of this Elamite helmet, which was probably worn by a high-ranking official.

Yet out of Sumer's remains another important civilization arose. Babylonia, a barely known Sumerian city-state before the Amorite takeover, grew extremely powerful under the new regime. It eventually dominated the region, and in time the land once called Sumer came to be known as Babylonia.

Babylonia developed its own culture, but its regional supremacy did not go unchallenged. At various times it was overrun by hostile powers. In the ninth century B.C. its northern Mesopotamian neighbor Assyria even imposed its rule on Babylonia.

For a while the Babylonians managed to overthrow their oppressors. But the situation changed in 539 B.C. with the invasion of Cyrus, king of Persia (now Iran). As Cyrus quickly proved himself a fair and unoppressive leader, the backlash against him was neither very strong nor widespread. Before long Babylonia simply blended into the Persian empire, never again to emerge as an independent nation.

Since then the area has been occupied by a number of other powers, including the Greeks, Arabs, and Turks. During World War I the British defeated the Turks and gained control

In ancient times, the city of Nippur,
the ruins of which are shown here,
was surrounded not by desert but by
vast irrigated fields.

of the region. They renamed the land Iraq and set up a British-controlled Arab government. But pressured by a growing internal Iraqi freedom movement, the British finally granted Iraq its independence in 1932.

The southeastern portion of modern-day Iraq includes the territory that was Sumer. But while its influence may be felt in many ways, the only hard evidence we have of this ancient culture comes from archaeological digs. As an ancient Sumerian poet summed up the fleeting nature of society and civilization:

Only the gods live forever....

As for mankind, numbered are their days.

Whatever they achieve is but wind.[5]

IMPORTANT DATES

3500 B.C.	The Sumerians settle the marshy area near the Persian Gulf later known as Sumer.
3000 B.C.	Sumer is made up of more than a dozen cities that function independently as separate states.
2600 B.C.	Gilgamesh, an epic figure in Sumerian legends, rules the city-state of Erech.
2250 B.C.	Sumer is overrun by the Gutians—a barbarian horde from the north.
2120 B.C.	Sumerian leader Utuhegal drives out the barbarous Gutians. After only seven years in power he is overthrown by one of his generals, Ur-Nammu.

2100 B.C.	Ur-Nammu proves to be a strong leader who starts a line of able rulers.
2094 B.C.	Shulgi, Ur-Nammu's son, rules for more than forty years, making advances in art and technology as well as devising Sumer's first legal code.
2028 B.C.	During Ibbi-Sin's reign Sumerian power begins to crumble. He is forced to face enemy attacks on more than one front while dealing with numerous disloyal army generals and city-state governors.
2006 B.C.	Sumer, overtaken by invaders, ceases to be a distinct power.

NOTES

1. Arthur Cotterell, ed., *The Encyclopedia of Civilizations* (New York: Mayflower Books, Inc., 1980), p. 72.

2. Samuel Noah Kramer and The Editors of Time-Life Books, Inc., *Cradle of Civilization* (Alexandria, VA: Time-Life Books, 1978), p. 35.

3. Samuel Noah Kramer, *The Sumerians: Their History, Culture, and Character* (Chicago: The University of Chicago Press, 1963), p. 232.

4. Jack M. Sasson, ed., *Civilizations of the Ancient Near East* (New York: Charles Scribner's Sons, 1995), p. 198.

5. Special Publications Division, National Geographic Society, *Splendors of the Past: Lost Cities of the Ancient World* (Washington, D.C.: National Geographic Society, 1981), p. 36.

GLOSSARY

affluent–wealthy; well-to-do

archaeologist–a person who studies ancient cultures chiefly by digging up and examining remains (tools, pottery, jewelry, etc.)

astronomy–the study of the stars, moon, planets, and other bodies in space

barbarian–a member of a tribe or group considered uncivilized

botany–the study of plant life

chariot–an ancient two-wheeled horse-drawn vehicle used in war or for racing

cuneiform script–a method of writing developed by the Sumerians in which a series of picture symbols are used to represent both living and nonliving things

deity–god

domesticated–tamed

flax–a plant used in making linen

fowler–a person who hunts wild game birds

irrigation–a means through which water is channeled to arid (dry) land

marsh–a swampland area

mausoleum–a large tomb

nomadic–moving from place to place; wandering

offspring–children

peninsula–an area of land jutting out from the mainland that is surrounded by water on three sides

reservoir–a reserve of water

ritual–a religious ceremony or rite

shade gardening–planting a garden in the shade of tall trees to shield it from harsh weather conditions

silt–fine particles of earth sediment in water

stylus–an ancient wedge-shaped instrument used for writing on clay tablets

ziggurat–an ancient pyramid-shaped terraced tower on which a temple was built

FURTHER READING

Avi-Yonah, Michael. *Dig This! How Archaeologists Uncover Our Past.* Minneapolis: Runestone Press, 1993.

Ayoub, Abderrahman. *Umm El Madayan: An Islamic City Through the Ages.* Boston: Houghton Mifflin, 1994.

Bailey, Jill, and Tony Sedden. *The Young Oxford Book of the Prehistoric World.* New York: Oxford University Press, 1996.

Beckwith, Carol, and Angela Fisher. *African Ark: People and the Ancient Cultures of Ethiopia and the Horn of Africa.* New York: Abrams, 1993.

Charley, Catherine. *Tombs & Treasures.* New York: Viking, 1995.

Corbishley, Mike. *Secret Cities.* New York: Lodestar Books, 1989.

Facchini, Fiorenzo. *Humans: Origins and Evolution.* Chatham, NJ: Raintree/Steck-Vaughn, 1995.

Goldenstern, Joyce. *Lost Cities.* Cliffside, NJ: Enslow, 1966.

Gonen, Rivka. *Fired Up! Making Pottery in Ancient Times.* Minneapolis: Lerner, 1993.

Hackwell, W. John. *Digging Up the Past.* New York: Charles Scribner's Sons, 1986.

Jenkins, Earnestine. *A Glorious Past: Ancient Egypt, Ethiopia and Nubia.* New York: Chelsea House, 1995.

Marston, Elsa. *The Ancient Egyptians.* Tarrytown, NY: Benchmark Books, 1995.

Platt, Richard. *The Smithsonian Visual Timeline of Inventions.* New York: Dorling Kindersley, 1994.

Putnam, James, and Jeremy Pemberton. *Amazing Facts About Ancient Egypt.* New York: Abrams, 1995.

INDEX

Adoption, 29
Amorites, 48-50
Arabian Peninsula, 15
Archaeologists, 12, 47, 52
Architecture, 12, 17, 18, 39
Arts, 12, 47
Assyria, 12, 50
Astronomy, 12, 37, 47

Babylonia, 12, 50
Basket makers, 43
Beer, 44, 45
Botany, 37
Burial, 20-21, 30, 47

Canals, 19
Carpenters, 43
Chariots, 21, 43
Children, 10, 29
Cities, 17, 21-22, 28

Clothing, 29-31
"Cradle of civilization," 12, 13
Craftspeople, 42-44
Crops, 10, 14, 39-40
Cuneiform script, 33-35
Cyrus, king of Persia, 50

Deities (gods), 17
Discipline, 35
Divorce, 29
Doctors, 44, 47
Domesticated farm animals, 43-44

Education, 35, 37
Elamites, 24, 48, 49
Erech, 23-24, 26
Etana, King, 22-23
Euphrates River, 10, 14, 17

Family life, 29

Farming, 10, 14, 15, 19, 26-27, 39-40
Fishing, 44
Food, 43, 44
Fowlers, 44
Furniture, 32, 43

Game birds, 44
Gilgamesh, King, 24-26
Government, 19, 20
Grave sites, 20-21, 47
Gutians, 24, 26, 28

Headdresses, 46, 47
Hercules, 24
Houses, 15, 30

Ibbi-Sin, King, 48-49
Intermarriage, 15
Inventions, 12, 39, 40
Iran, 15, 50
Iraq, 50, 52
Irrigation, 14, 19, 39, 47
Isin, 37, 49

Jewelry, 30, 46, 47
Judges, 37

Kish, 22, 24

Land ownership, 28
Leaders, 20-28
Leather workers, 43
Legal system, 12, 28, 37-38
Linen, 41
Lipit-Ishtar, King, 37

Literature, 12, 37

Marriage, 29
Mathematics, 12, 37, 47
Medicine, 12, 37, 44, 47
Mesopotamia, 10, 12
Metalworkers, 42-43
Music, 47

Nippur, 51
Noah, 15

Occupations, 29

Persia, 50
Persian Gulf, 10, 14, 17
Pottery, 14
Priesthood, 17

Religion, 17

Science, 44, 47
Scribes, 33, 35, 37
Semitic tribes, 15
Shade gardening, 40
Sheep, 41, 43-44
Shem, 15
Ships, 41, 43
Shulgi, King, 28, 36, 37
Slaves, 20, 21, 29, 38
Social reforms, 27
Soldiers, 21
Spoils of war, 22-23
Stylus, 33
Sumer
    architecture, 17, 18, 39

Sumer *(continued)*
    arts, 47
    cities, 17, 21-22, 28
    clothing, 29-31
    craftspeople, 42-44
    education, 35, 37
    family life, 29
    farming, 15, 19, 26-27, 39-40
    food, 43, 44
    furniture, 32, 43
    government, 19, 20
    grave sites, 20-21, 47
    houses, 15, 30
    land ownership, 28
    leaders, 20-28
    legal system, 28, 37-38
    medicine, 37, 44, 47
    origins of, 15
    religion, 17
    science, 44, 47
    technology, 39, 40
    trade and commerce, 32, 33, 39-41
    warfare, 19-21, 23, 24, 28, 48-49
    women, 29, 38
    writing system, 33-35

Syrian Desert, 15

Technology, 12, 39, 40
Temples, 17-19, 28
Tigris River, 10, 12, 14, 17
Trade and commerce, 32, 33, 39-41

Ubaidians, 14-15
Ur, 22-24, 26, 27
Ur-Nammu, King, 26-28, 48
Utuhegal, King, 26

Veterinarians, 47

Wandering groups, 9
Warfare, 19-21, 23, 24, 28, 48-50
Water rights, 19
Weapons, 42-43
Wheel, invention of, 12, 39, 40
Women, 10, 29, 38
Wood, 41-43
Wool production, 41
Writing system, 33-35

Ziggurats, 17, 18